ALL ABOARD AMERICA

Empire State Building

ABDO
Publishing Company

A *Buddy* Book
by
Sarah Tieck

VISIT US AT
www.abdopublishing.com

Published by ABDO Publishing Company, 8000 West 78th Street, Edina, Minnesota 55439.

Copyright © 2008 by Abdo Consulting Group, Inc. International copyrights reserved in all countries. No part of this book may be reproduced in any form without written permission from the publisher. Buddy Books™ is a trademark and logo of ABDO Publishing Company.

Printed in the United States.

Contributing Editor: Michael P. Goecke
Graphic Design: Deborah Coldiron
Cover Photograph: Photos.com
Interior Photographs/Illustrations: Getty Images (pages 6, 7, 17, 21); Photos.com (pages 5, 10, 13, 19); TongRo Image Stock (pages 9, 15, 22)

Library of Congress Cataloging-in-Publication Data

Tieck, Sarah, 1976-
    Empire State Building / Sarah Tieck.
        p. cm. — (All aboard America)
    Includes bibliographical references and index.
    ISBN 978-1-59928-935-9
    1. Empire State Building (New York, N.Y.)—Juvenile literature. 2. New York (N.Y.)—Buildings, structures, etc.—Juvenile literature. I. Title.

F128.8.E46T54 2008
974.7'1—dc22
                                                            2007027264

Table of Contents

The Empire State Building is a 102-story skyscraper in New York City, New York. It is also a famous part of New York City's skyline.

The Empire State Building was completed in 1931. Since then, many people have visited it. From its top, they can see an excellent view of New York City!

The Empire State Building is about 1,454 feet (443 m) tall. Its name was inspired by New York's state nickname, the Empire State.

When it was built, the Empire State Building was considered an important accomplishment. At that time, it was the tallest building in the world. Today, it is the tallest building in New York City!

Construction began on March 17, 1930. Workers completed the Empire State Building in just 410 days!

The building was part of a competition between Walter Chrysler

and John Jakob Raskob. These businessmen were trying to see who could construct the tallest building.

This display shows the height difference between the Chrysler Building *(left)* and the Empire State Building *(right)*.

The Chrysler Building was finished first. At that time, it was tallest. But, the Empire State Building soon became the tallest building in both the city and the world.

There were about 3,400 workers involved in constructing the Empire State Building at one time. Some of them worked high above the ground.

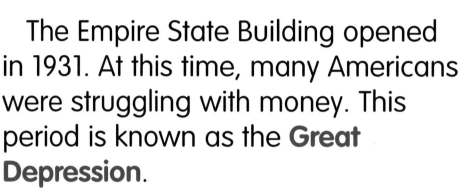

The Empire State Building opened in 1931. At this time, many Americans were struggling with money. This period is known as the **Great Depression**.

Because of this, many of the building's offices were empty. People even started calling it the "Empty State Building"!

During its early years, the building did not make much money. It wasn't until 1950 that the building began making a profit!

Today, the Empire State Building is a New York City Landmark and a National Historic Landmark.

The Empire State Building is made of glass, steel, and stone. A **spire** sits on top of its 102 stories.

The Empire State Building is an example of Art Deco **architecture**. Art Deco was a popular design style from 1920 to 1940.

Art Deco designs use **geometric** shapes, **setbacks**, and bold colors. They also feature materials such as chrome.

Empire State Building

Spire

Chysler Building

Setbacks

It is easy to see Art Deco influences in the Empire State Building's exterior. The spire is an Art Deco design, and the building features setbacks.

The Empire State Building is a very strong building. It weighs about 365,000 tons (331,000 t)!

The Empire State Building is made of about 10 million bricks. Building materials also included limestone, marble, glass, and steel. There are 6,500 windows. And, the building has about 70 miles (110 km) of pipes.

The cost of the building and its land was $40,948,900. The building alone cost $24,718,000 to construct.

The Empire State Building's spire is 16 stories tall!

People enter the Empire State Building through a three-story lobby. The lobby features bridges made of glass and stainless steel.

The first 85 floors of the building contain **commercial** and office spaces. The 86th and 102nd floors are observatories.

At one time, there were 67 elevators. But today, visitors can enter the office tower on one of 73 elevators.

There is also a famous piece of **aluminum** art that shows the Empire State Building. The building is pictured without its antenna, because that wasn't added until 1952.

The Empire State Building's address is 350 Fifth Avenue in New York. The lobby is one of its most famous parts of the building.

The Empire State Building is famous for its observatories. People can take special high-speed elevators to these areas. There, they can look out over the city.

The 86th-floor observatory is 1,050 feet (320 m) above the ground. People can see New York City from every angle. From the 86th floor, they can go to the enclosed 102nd floor. This is 1,224 feet (373 m) high!

About 110 million people have visited the observatories. These areas are open every day of the year from 8 AM to 2 AM!

The 86th floor is famous for its role in two movies. It was featured in *An Affair to Remember* and *Sleepless in Seattle*.

CHAPTER 7

Night Lights

Lighting is an important feature of the Empire State Building. Its many lights shine through the windows at night. But, the Empire State Building is known for its special lighting.

In 1932, a light atop the Empire State Building could be seen for 50 miles (80 km). This signal let people know Franklin D. Roosevelt was elected president.

And in 1964, floodlights were placed on the outside of the building. They cover the building in light at night. They change colors for different events and holidays.

Most nights, the Empire State Building glows white in the sky. Red and green celebrate Christmas, while red, white, and blue mark Independence Day and other events.

Detour ⬇

Did You Know?

. . . From 1931 to 1972, the Empire State Building was the tallest building in the world!

. . . Today, the Empire State Building is the second-tallest building in the United States. And, it is still one of the ten tallest buildings in the world!

. . . The Empire State Building has been featured in many movies. One of the most famous movies is *King Kong* in 1933.

. . . In the 1800s, a farm was located on the land where the Empire State Building now stands. After John Thompson sold his farm, one of New York's wealthiest families bought the land. They built mansions and hotels on it. One of the most famous hotels was the Waldorf-Astoria Hotel.

Actress Fay Wray is famous for her role in *King Kong*.

CHAPTER 8

Empire State Building Today

Today, the Empire State Building still ranks among the tallest buildings in the world. Also, it remains a favorite New York City **landmark**.

Over the years, millions of people have visited its famous observatories. And, many more visit each day!

Today, the Empire State Building houses about 1,000 businesses with 20,000 employees. It is one of the busiest office buildings in the United States!

Important Words

aluminum a silvery-white metallic material.

architecture the art and science of planning and designing buildings.

commercial pertaining to business.

geometric consisting of basic shapes, such as circles and squares.

Great Depression the period from 1929 to 1942 when many U.S. citizens were unemployed and very poor.

landmark a feature that is easily recognized.

setback an architectural feature that resembles a series of steps.

spire a tall tower that comes to a point.

WEB SITES

To learn more about the Empire State Building, visit ABDO Publishing Company on the World Wide Web. Web sites about The Empire State Building are featured on our Book Links page. These links are routinely monitored and updated to provide the most current information available.

www.abdopublishing.com

Index